IN A HEARTBEAT

*A journey of hope and healing
for those who have lost a baby*

DAWN SIEGRIST WALTMAN

Faithful Woman, an imprint of
Cook Communications Ministries,
Colorado Springs, CO 80918
Cook Communications, Paris, Ontario
Kingsway Communications, Eastbourne, England

In a Heartbeat
©2002 by Dawn Siegrist Waltman
All rights reserved.

1 2 3 4 5 6 7 8 9 10 Printing/Year 06 05 04 03 02

Senior Editor: Janet Lee
Editor: Marianne Hering
Cover photo by EyeWire, Inc.
Cover design by Sandy Flewelling

SPECIAL THANKS

Darla Joy ... *one of the dearest friends a person could be blessed with. What can I say to sum up all you have meant to me? Thank you for believing in my dreams and for helping to make them come true.*

My "little sister" **Sharon** ... *your constant reassurance and genuine excitement for this dream will always hold a special place in my heart.*

My faithful prayer warriors **Kelly, Jessica, Kim, Michele, and Dawn** ... *what an encouragement and inspiration you have been to me! Without your faithful prayers, this message of hope and healing would never have had the power to reach so many.*

Janet Lee *of Cook Communications* ... *thank you for understanding and caring about the hearts of people who have lost their precious children. Your professionalism and sensitive spirit have blessed this project in so many ways.*

And finally to **Brian** ... *the love of my life and the awesome daddy of our children, both on earth and in heaven. God gave me the best when He gave me you! I love you!*

DEDICATION

I dedicate this book to the Lord Jesus Christ. Without Him as my personal Lord and Savior there would be no message of hope and healing to share.

In a Heartbeat is merely a reflection of the work He has done in my life. For this reason, I must acknowledge Him as the true author of this book. With open hands and an open heart, I lay this book before Jesus Christ and ask Him to use it to touch the lives of hurting women. May He, and only He, receive all the honor and glory.

Dawn Waltman, 2002

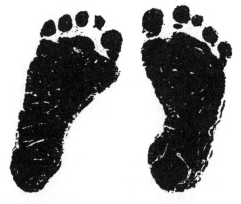

Molly's precious footprints

In Memory

Molly Dawn Waltman
March 25, 1996

Although you never saw the sunshine outside
of your mommy's womb, your little life
touched the lives of so many … bringing hope,
healing, and the promise of heaven.

I love you, little Molly,
and I will never forget you.

And in memory of my two precious
babies, Mitchell and Madison, my
tiny rosebuds, carried to heaven
just weeks after your little
lives had begun.

Oh, how I long for the day
when I will see you in full bloom.
Please know that I love you forever.

CONTENTS

LETTER TO A
GRIEVING MOTHER

Dear friend,

Although you may not know it, I have been praying for you. Years before this book was in print, I prayed for each hurting mother who would someday hold these meditations in her hands. In addition, women's groups, home groups, and countless individuals have prayed and are praying as you move through this grief-filled journey. Angels have been called forth on your behalf. They are surrounding you right now, protecting you and ministering to you. God loves you so much. He hurts with you and wants to carry you in His arms.

I wrote *In a Heartbeat* because God placed in my heart a desire to meet a need in the lives of grieving women who suffer the loss of their children through miscarriage, stillbirth, or early infant death. Eight years ago, I lost two babies to miscarriages. Five years later, my little girl Molly was stillborn at twenty weeks. It was such a painful and confusing time. As a result of these losses, God gave me the vision to create a book that would actually serve as a companion for grieving mothers. *In a Heartbeat* is that vision.

These meditations are based on my journey of grief, hope, and healing after Molly's death. They reflect the many hills, valleys, and plateaus that I encountered during that first and most difficult year. The sole purpose of this resource is to reassure mothers they are not alone in their feelings of sorrow, anger, and confusion—and neither are they alone in hope of joy, love, and healing.

The meditations are not dated, so turn to them whenever you need to feel the companionship, understanding, and hope of someone who has traveled this difficult journey. Some readings focus on a specific event, occasion, or struggle that may be particularly difficult that first year. Review the meditation titles so that when a particular event in your life seems exceptionally hard, you can turn to a reflection that will help you feel the sun again. It is unlikely that you will identify with every meditation, but my prayer is that you will be able to identify with many.

God's Word is so awesome. For this reason, each meditation contains a verse that has the power to reach where healing will begin, to the very core of your being. The days and weeks that initially surround the death of your baby will no doubt be filled with the prayers of faithful people. It is in the months that follow that a woman often struggles with loneliness and feels that the world is bleak. Although each meditation is based on my heartache three years ago, the prayer at the bottom of each entry is one that I am praying for you today. Please know I am committed to interceding and praying on your behalf.

In Jesus' love,
Dawn

The Cords of Death

The cords of death entangled me,
the anguish of the grave came upon me;
I was overcome by trouble and sorrow.
—Psalm 116:3

*M*y eyes searched the screen, desperately looking for the pulse of my baby's heartbeat. Only six weeks earlier I had watched with fascination as sonogram waves showed the baby inside my womb, rolling, kicking, and stretching. Now that same figure was still. A lump formed in my throat as I choked out the words: "My baby's not moving. My baby is dead, isn't it?"

The doctor swept the silver ball over my swollen stomach. I watched his eyes as he concentrated on the screen.

The doctor knew the answer. My husband knew the answer. And I knew the answer before I had even asked the question. My husband gripped my hand as dark thoughts and emotions swept over me. "Oh God, no! Please, no!" I cried. My body shook with uncontrollable sobs as I realized what the motionless figure on the screen meant. My baby, my precious baby was dead.

Dear friend,
I am so sorry your baby has died. I desperately wish I could change what has happened. I have felt your pain, so please know I care and I am praying for you. Right now, let God carry you. He won't let go of you. I promise.

OF LIFE AND LOVE

These three remain: faith, hope and love.
… the greatest of these is love.
—1 Corinthians 13:13

*T*he cold morning air stung my face as I walked to the car in a daze. My mind and body felt numb. It was only a little more than twelve hours since I had found out the baby had died. Now, here I was going to the hospital to give birth. An overwhelming feeling of sorrow and regret stirred in my chest and spread throughout my body. "I have nothing to give you, little baby. I'm so sorry!" I cried. "No special stuffed animal, no tiny sweater, no flower, nothing." What kind of mother was I to have nothing, not a single thing, to give my precious baby?

Time seemed to stand still as I cried in the darkness of the morning. As my tears slowly subsided, I felt a voice inside my heart. Not an audible voice, but the voice of God's Spirit. The voice was unmistakably clear. "You have nothing to give your child … but no 'thing' can compare to what you did give. You gave your baby life and you gave your baby love. Nothing is more precious than those gifts."

Dear friend,

I know you love your baby so much. I pray that you would know that the gift of life and the gift of love are the greatest gifts your baby ever desired.

No Place to Run

My heart is in anguish within me;
the terrors of death assail me....
Oh, that I had the wings of a dove!
I would fly away and be at rest.
–Psalm 55:4, 6

As the nurse pushed the wheelchair into my hospital room, my husband and I knew it was time to say good-bye to our little girl. I had been so strong throughout the evening, but now I wanted to run away and hide. My emotions buckled and collapsed when I found there was nowhere to go.

The reality of leaving Molly and never seeing her again on earth was the most heart-wrenching feeling I have ever experienced.

Brian and I wrapped her hospital blanket snugly around her little body, trying to remember every detail of her tiny face. After several minutes, I finally kissed her forehead and laid her down. She looked so small and vulnerable lying on that big bed. I kept my eyes on the little bundle as the nursed pushed my wheelchair out of the room. I turned my body around, trying desperately to keep Molly in my sight as long as I could. In a couple of seconds, though, we were out of the door, and my little girl was out of my reach.

When I left Molly in that room, I left part of my heart with her. I would never be the same again.

Dear friend,

It's OK to want to cling to your child and at the same time to feel like running away from the pain of separation. It hurts so much to lose your child. But as you run, run into the arms of Jesus. Cling to Him. He wants to hold you close.

Hold My Hand

I am the Lord your God. I am holding your right hand.
And I tell you, "Don't be afraid. I will help you."
—Isaiah 41:13

*T*he first few days after Molly's death I clung desperately to my husband. He answered the phone, he answered the door, and he literally answered everyone's questions. He made arrangements with the funeral director, our pastor, and the support-committee members at church. I held his hand and he led me through the events that surrounded the death of our little girl.

Before long, however, he had to go back to work and there was no longer a hand to hold. Suddenly the world around me seemed so very, very big. The phone calls, the visitors, the cards and letters, the flowers, the tears, the emotions and the never-ending questions swirled around and around in my head, creating even more fear and confusion in my already upside-down world. I needed someone to hold my hand. Someone whom I could trust to gently lead me through the chaos of my everyday life, through my pain and fear, and through my journey of overwhelming grief.

Dear friend,

God promises in His Word that He is there to hold your hand through this difficult journey. Don't be afraid. He will help you. My prayer is that you will reach out to the hand that is reaching out to you.

RESURRECTION POWER

For the Lord himself will come down from heaven,
with a loud command, with the voice of the archangel
and with the trumpet call of God,
and the dead in Christ will rise first.
—1 Thessalonians 4:16

*T*he sun was bright and the air crisp and cool as we gathered at the gravesite. Our pastor laid his hand on the tiny white casket and with boldness and assurance spoke these words:

> *"For as much as the spirit has departed this body, we do commit all that is mortal of our sister to its resting place in the earth. But the spirit of our sister, which is the true person, we commit to God, who alone knows the secrets of the resurrection and life eternal. Knowing that at the second coming of Jesus, the dead in Christ shall rise first and we who are alive and remain will be caught up with them in the clouds to meet the Lord in the air."*

I was totally caught off guard at the thought of our baby breaking out of the grave with a new body. Sure, I believed in the resurrection of God's people, but I had never given thought to how that promise applied to Molly. An awesome feeling of God's power washed over me as I took a moment and entertained that very thought. The new body of our Molly, breaking out of the very spot where we were standing! What an incredible promise.

Dear friend,

It's true! Because of God's power, you and I will both see our babies again. Hallelujah! I pray with all my heart that you would know and take joy in that promise today!

RECKLESS WORDS

Reckless words pierce like a sword.
—Proverbs 12:18

*W*ell, look at it this way, there was probably something wrong with the baby anyway." "You are still young; you can have more children." "Be thankful you have other children."

I had been warned I would hear comments like these. I thought I was prepared. But when I heard those word with my own ears, they pierced my heart. I stared at the person speaking to me and thought to myself, *You have no idea what you're talking about!*

It doesn't matter if my baby had a birth defect or not. She was my child. And I was her mother. Do people think I would love her less if she was not perfect?

So what if I am young and can possibly have more children? What does that have to do with the death of *this* child? Sometimes I want to say, "Don't you get it? This was not an appliance that didn't work and I can return for a replacement. This was a baby—my baby. And now my baby is dead."

Dear friend,

I pray that our Lord Jesus would protect your heart by allowing all reckless words to fall on deaf ears.

BURDENS OF SORROW—
MESSAGES OF LOVE

Carry each other's burdens.
—Galatians 6:2

I stare at the little pile of envelopes on the kitchen counter not knowing whether to look at the cards inside. I treasure the thoughts and prayers from people, but there is something unsettling about the cards, because they also convey, well—sympathy. Which obviously means something sad happened. Like the death of a loved one. My loved one. My baby.

Fingering the glued envelopes, I am amazed at the power these little pieces of paper hold. While it's true each card serves as a reminder of what death has stolen from me, I understand each one also serves to bring a message of hope, a message of empathy, and a message of love. Someone took the time to care and to share my pain. In essence, the senders are taking some of my burden of sorrow on their own hearts. I can either accept their gift and allow my load to be lightened or I can push them away and struggle on by myself. The choice is mine.

Dear friend,

There is much pain and grief surrounding the death of your baby, but God has given other people the miraculous power to share some of your heartache. Don't keep it all to yourself, for it will destroy your very being. Allow others to carry a portion of your pain if they so desire. Your heart depends on it.

FREEDOM TO GRIEVE

And let us consider one another how we may spur one
another on toward love and good deeds.
—Hebrews 10:24

I lay across the bed sobbing at the rawness of my pain. It hurt so much. Mingled in with the grief was a stab of bitterness as I listened to the buzz of my husband's power tools. Three days earlier our baby had died. Three days! So why was he "up and at 'em" as if nothing happened? Where were the signs of his pain and his grief? Didn't he understand what we had lost? Or was he so preoccupied with the construction project that he had already forgotten about our baby? The addition itself was even a source of pain. We had started the project because our family was expanding and we needed more room. So much for expanding!

Suddenly, I realized the tools were silent. I heard the floor creak and looked up to see Brian coming into the room. He walked over to the bed, sat down, and held me tightly. I blurted out my accusations and waited for his defense. When I looked up into his face, I saw tears brimming in his eyes. Instantly, I realized what a foolish mistake I had made. After nine years of marriage, how could I have doubted my husband's love for our little girl?

For the next half hour or so we talked about our differences in grieving. As a woman, I needed time to be still, to think, and to cry in order to process my emotions. As a man, my husband needed to keep moving, keep going, keep plowing ahead with a task or physical labor in order to work through the emotions that swirled around in his head.

I rested in his arms and realized that together we had made it through yet another step in our journey of grief.

Dear friend,

My prayer is that as you and your husband sort out the thoughts, feelings, and emotions surrounding the death of your baby, you would give one another the freedom to grieve, each in your own way. May God's grace be upon you so that this process draws you together instead of tearing you apart.

THE ROSE BUSH

by Joylynn Charity Miller

Once, a little rose bush,
With no blooms yet to bear,
Inched itself toward a picket fence,
And quietly rested there.

Then day by day it pulled its stems,
To the flaws in the fence's wall,
And slowly crept its way …
Until it wasn't there at all.

On the other side it flourished,
On the other side, grew lush,
But the planter of the seedling,
Missed that beautiful rose bush.

So young and it had vanished,
So small and it was gone,
But on the other side of the fence,
It still, to life, held on!

And as the little babies here,
Have left without a trace,
They rest upon the heavenly shore,
And bloom in all God's grace!

Joylynn Miller, age 14, from Ukiah, California, penned this beautiful poem as a gift to her friend who had suffered the loss of her baby.

A Teardrop on Earth

You put my tears in your bottle; are they not in your book?
—*Psalm 56:8 (NASB)*

Grief has become so commonplace in my life it almost feels like a companion. No, not a friend, but a companion whose constant presence makes me wonder if I'll ever live without tears or "him."

I've been told when a person cries, endorphins are released in his or her body, serving as a natural sedative to calm the mind and body. Even in the midst of grief, I find that scientific trivia amazing. The human body is indeed an incredible miracle, right down to crying. And while I am thankful for the endorphins that no doubt help sustain my physical and mental state, I often wonder if there isn't something more to the tears that overflow from the reservoirs of my aching heart.

Today I found the connection. A dear friend sent a beautiful card with a single teardrop and these powerful words, *"A teardrop on earth summons the King of heaven"* (Charles Swindoll). Oh, how my heart sang! God cares about my tears. He sees and feels each and every one. Psalm 56:8 reveals that God even collects my tears in a bottle. Maybe it's not an actual glass bottle; more likely, I believe it's a special crevice in His heart.

Dear friend,

I pray in the weeks, months, and even years following the death of your baby you won't be afraid to cry. The King of heaven sees your tears and treasures them in His own heart.

ROADWAY IN THE WILDERNESS

"I will even make a roadway in the wilderness."
—Isaiah 43:19 (NASB)

I certainly did not make reservations for the journey of grief I took following Molly's death. To think pain would not be over in a day or two made me feel like I wanted to crawl in a hole. With no "itinerary" I could not know what emotions, situations, or circumstances I might face tomorrow—or even six months ahead. My heart ached, the "baggage" of mourning was too heavy, and my trip had just begun.

I understand now why grief journeys are referred to as "wilderness experiences." Feelings of isolation, emptiness, and loneliness were all too familiar; nothing seemed able to nourish my aching spirit. Accomplishing simple daily tasks was as difficult as fighting off a wild beast. Communicating with others was like forging through a river. One Sunday, however, a single phrase from a praise song based on Isaiah 49:13 breathed hope into my soul: "Behold I will do something new among you ... I will even make a roadway in the wilderness ... " God would make a way when there seemed to be no way. He would make a roadway through this barren, desolate wilderness.

So what was I to do? Follow! Follow the roadway. Follow Him one step at a time through the twists and turns and over the hills and valleys of this wilderness until I reach the lushness of the promised land that He has prepared just for me.

Dear friend,

God has not abandoned you on this journey. Follow Him, one step at a time, one day at a time, through the wilderness. I promise a lush land awaits you, offering peace, hope, healing, and joy.

HEAVEN?

And if I go and prepare a place for you,
vill come back and take you to be with me
that you also may be where I am.
—John 14:3

*H*eaven. Everybody is talking about it. Everybody is telling me my baby is alive and happy in heaven. I hang on to the hope of seeing her again in heaven. At least I want to hang on to that hope. The problem is, heaven seems so far away, so mystical, so intangible, so ... unbelievable. But I am a Christian. Why do I doubt? Why does this place suddenly seem like nothing more than wishful thinking?

Oh, God, I can't live like this. My heart desperately wants to cling to the hope of heaven, but my brain and my gut are tumbling over and over with questions. I want my belief in heaven and my belief in You to be so strong, so unwavering, so real that it changes the way I live, think, and feel. I want hope to eclipse the fear and terror that strangles my heart. God I need You. I need all of You right now in the midst of this turmoil. Help me, Jesus.

Dear friend,

Times like this are filled with doubt, fear, and questioning. Please don't hide these emotions and feelings. I pray you would seek out a trusted friend who will lift you up in prayer and with whom you can share your struggles. God will meet you right where you are. I promise.

MISSING YOU

For He is our God.
And we are the people of His pasture,
and the sheep of His hand.
—Psalm 95:7 (NASB)

Dear Little Baby, how often I sit quietly, alone with my thoughts of you. There is just so much I wonder about. How would our lives have been different if you had not died? I miss your smile. A smile that I have never seen and yet, how I miss it! I wish you could tell me, Sweet Baby, what color is your hair and your pretty little eyes? What about your personality? Are you a little ball of lightning or are you more quiet and shy?

Oh, how I long to have you with me! I look out at the evening sky and I see the magnificence of God's power as He paints a spectacular picture for all to see. As I watch the sky change, I feel a closeness to you. Maybe because it draws me closer to the God who holds the answers to my wondering thoughts. And closer to the God who holds you.

Dear friend,

I know you miss your baby terribly. So many questions about your child roll around in your head with no one to provide the answers in this lifetime. Though you may not know the answers to some of your questions until you meet your baby in heaven, God still wants to give you the precious gift of peace. Peace in knowing your little lamb is resting in the hand of God and being cared for by the Shepherd Himself.

A LONELY HEART

You are intimately acquainted with all my ways.
—Psalm 139:3 (NASB)

I want to talk about Molly, but no one is here to listen. I wonder what she may have looked like had she lived and blossomed. What would her personality have been like had she had the chance to grow outside my womb? What would she have accomplished had her feet ever walked on this earth?

I want to talk about Molly and form a clearer image in my heart and mind as to who she really is. My husband asks "what's the point" since it's all speculation. *But is it?* Maybe God wants to give us a glimpse into Molly's heart.

Brian is at peace knowing she is in heaven, and he is content with memories. Sometimes I wish I could accept what little we have of Molly—the memories and the hope of heaven—and leave it at that. But there are times when I would love to have Brian join me on one of my "journeys of wonderment" when my little girl is as close as my heart.

Dear friend,

Even with the comforting support of family and friends, there are times when the journey of a broken heart is painfully lonely. Don't be embarrassed by the dreams and flights of imagination that fill your mind. God created your heart, mind, and soul in His image. He sees those "journeys of wonderment" and longs to travel with you.

HEALING WORDS

The tongue of the wise brings healing.
—*Proverbs 12:18*

"I am so sorry you lost Molly."

"My heart breaks for your loss."

"I just wanted you to know I am thinking about you."

The tongue has the power to tear down or build up. While many careless words were thrown my way after Molly died, there were also many healing words. It sounds so good to hear Molly's name spoken by someone other than family members. I also like to hear comments and phrases acknowledging my loss as that of a real child.

One friend simply held me and said, "I just don't know what to say, but I hurt so much for you." Her words were like ointment on an open sore.

I am thankful God continues to bring people into my life who seek His wisdom and speak words that bring healing to my broken heart.

Dear friend,

My prayer is that you would feel God's healing power through the wise words of compassionate friends.

I CAN'T FIX IT

The battle is not yours, but God's.
—2 Chronicles 20:15

*A*s both a husband and a father, Brian takes great delight and satisfaction in fixing everything from a squeaky door to a broken toy. I can't count the times I have heard the words, "It's OK Mommy, Daddy can fix it," after I have failed to repair something for my children.

Today, I asked Brian what emotion or issue he struggles with the most since losing Molly. He didn't have to think long before saying, "That I can't fix it. I can't make everything OK for you, for Matthew and Megan, and for me. I just can't." As those words tumbled from his mouth, I could sense the grip of helplessness that relentlessly held his heart captive. My eyes held his gaze and saw in his eyes the desperate struggle of being face-to-face with defeat. Our baby girl died without us even knowing it! A long journey of grief lie ahead of us with no option but to go through it. Brian was right. He couldn't fix this situation.

No amount of reassurance or encouragement would erase the struggle going on inside Brian. And just as I have my unique battles in this grief process, so Brian has his battles as well. This, I just learned, is one of them. I can do nothing by myself and yet I can do everything through Christ. By covering my husband in prayer and lifting him up before the Lord, I can rest assured God will meet him in the heat of this battle and see him through to victory.

Dear friend,

Your spouse will work through battles that belong only to him just as you will work through battles that belong only to you. Cover him in prayer and know that while your struggles may be different, the heartache and sense of loss is the same.

CHRISTIAN PROFESSIONALS

He who pursues righteousness and love finds life,
prosperity and honor.
—Proverbs 21:21

I treasure the number of family members and friends who reached out in immeasurable ways during an incredibly difficult time in our lives. Beyond that intimate circle, I also feel blessed for the Christian professionals that God provided to minister to our family during our time of loss.

Our pastor and his wife came to the hospital as soon as they heard we were having a sonogram to determine if our baby had died. They were the first familiar faces we saw after the doctor confirmed that there were "no signs of a viable pregnancy." They hugged my husband and me and cried with us over the loss of our baby. Our pastor's words still echo in my mind. "No matter what, we will be here for you guys." And they were. The evening of Molly's birth, they came to the hospital again to hold our little girl. Two days later they guided us through the funeral service as we said good-bye to our tiny baby. We treasured them as our pastoral couple; even more so, we cherished them as friends.

My induced labor and delivery was a nightmare I thought I would not survive. But during those hours of anguish, God placed a compassionate Christian doctor by my bed. His words and actions revealed the work of God in his life. When our little girl was born, he blessed my heart by the way he gently held her and stroked her lifeless body. He knew our Molly was a precious child created in the image of God.

Six hours later we kissed our baby girl good-bye and laid her gently on the bed. Before we left, the nurse promised me they would not take Molly to the morgue, but would leave her on the bed until the undertaker came. When he came for Molly's body, he did not put her in a case or special box. Instead, he wrapped her snugly in a blanket and walked down the hall with her as if she were alive. The nurses all marveled at his incredible compassion. That very thought still warms my heart every time I think of it. Over the next several days, he took care of all the details surrounding the funeral and burial of Molly and never gave us a bill. We found out later he and his wife choose to do this regularly as a pro-life testimony.

We praise God for these men, not only for their professional skills, but more importantly for their ministry to hurting people. With grateful hearts we say "Thank you!" to the following Christian professionals and pray that God will richly bless each of them.

Pastor Marlin and Lisa Nafziger
of Bart Ministries, Christiana, PA

Dr. William Bradford
of Lancaster ObGyn Associates, Lancaster, PA

Steve Shivery
of Shivery Funeral Home, Christiana, PA

Dear friend,
Look around you and take note of the professional men and women that God has ordained to minister to you during this painful time. I pray you would be able to see these people as a gift from a God who cares about every detail of your difficult journey.

THE GIFT OF INTIMACY

Place me like a seal over your heart …
for love is as strong as death.
—Song of Songs 8:6

*D*uring these first weeks and months since Molly's death, I have realized how tense I feel over things that have always come so naturally before. Intimacy is one of those areas. Brian and I have always enjoyed a strong physical, emotional and sexual relationship. Our level of emotional and physical intimacy is growing even deeper since Molly's death. Praying together, sharing special thoughts, enjoying tight hugs and tender kisses all come easily and seem to be appropriate during our time of mourning.

Sexual intimacy, however, is a different story. There seems to be a hesitation that I can't quite describe. Brian feels uneasy and unsure, thinking he might possibly hurt me physically even though the doctor has said my body is recovering with no complications. He walks on eggshells, not knowing if his next step will crush the fragile emotional and physical heal-ing process. I feel uneasy and guilty, thinking that if I enjoy sexual intimacy then I somehow am betraying Molly. After all, if I am enjoying a special time with my husband then I must not hurt anymore. And if I don't hurt anymore then I must be over my grief of losing my baby. But that just isn't true!

My heart aches for my baby and yet I desire that special intimacy with my husband. Is it possible to feel both sets of emotions and yet stay true to my baby, my husband, and myself? I wish I knew.

Dear friend,

Sexual intimacy is a gift from God. A gift that celebrates your love for one another. The same love that miraculously breathed life into your child just a short time ago. I pray you would embrace that gift without hesitation. Don't let it slip away.

A Hole in My Heart

Incline Thine ear, O Lord, and answer me;
For I am afflicted and needy ...
To thee I cry all day long.
—Psalm 86:1, 3 (NASB)

There is a hole in my heart—a hole that some days feels so huge it could actually engulf me. It's a hole that came from losing Molly. It seems like when she died she took a part of my heart with her. In actuality, though, I gave her that part of me.

People around me know there's a hole in my heart. Sometimes I cry, sometimes I even chuckle to see how hard they try to fill it for me. Some of their attempts bless me, others irritate me. I know deep inside, though, they are doing it because they care about me.

I know I am going to be OK. I just need time. I need them to realize that pursuing a hobby, volunteering for a special project, taking a vacation, or even having another child will not fill that hole. Nothing will. As time passes and I continue to grow in God's grace, my heart will grow as well. As I love and am loved, my heart will grow even more. And as my heart steadily grows, the hole will seem smaller and to some degree less painful. But the hole and the ache that accompanies it will never go away. Nor do I want it to. For in that hole a glorious new hope will take root and be found.

Dear friend,

You know the pain and the deep ache the hole in your heart brings. My prayer is that God would show you the comfort and hope the hole can bring as well. Nothing on earth will ever fill that hole nor would you want it to. But cling to the promise of finding complete and total healing when you are ushered into heaven and reunited with the child who has for so long held that part of your heart.

The Hope of Heaven

*There will be no more death or mourning or crying
or pain, for the old order of things has passed away.*
—Revelation 21:4

$\mathcal{A}$s I walked out of the grocery store, I stopped to chat with an acquaintance I had met on a few occasions. After exchanging small talk, she smiled and asked excitedly, "So I guess you've had that little baby by now, haven't you?" Immediately I felt my entire body tighten as her words registered.

The story of a pregnant woman ends happily with the birth of a healthy baby. It's an exciting event for everyone, even mere acquaintances. The problem was, my pregnancy didn't have a storybook ending.

I shifted my bag of groceries and then quietly said, "Our baby died. She was stillborn." The woman's face immediately expressed sympathy for me. I knew she felt terrible for having asked the question and I felt terrible because she felt terrible! I hate when that happens.

As I walked home I thought about the

encounter. "Oh Molly, I miss you!" my heart cried.

God's promise of spending eternity with Molly doesn't always seem real to me. That day, however, it did. As I focused on the brilliant blue sky, I felt a closeness with God. Storybook endings don't always happen on earth, but I know God in His wisdom has written an ending to Molly's story that is truly "out of this world."

Dear friend,

When the promise of spending eternity with your baby seems so hard to believe, may you feel the power of God's presence so you can hang on to the hope of heaven.

Precious in His Sight

Precious in the sight of the Lord
Is the death of His godly ones.
—Psalm 116:15 (NASB)

*F*or quite a while after Molly died, I struggled with a question regarding her death. As a mother, the most painful thing to experience is the suffering of your child. The thought of my baby twisting and turning with pain before she died haunted me for weeks. How could I not have helped her? Worse yet, how could I not even have known she was in pain.

Finally I went to see the doctor who had delivered Molly. My voice trembled as I asked him the question I so desperately needed an answer to, "Did Molly suffer as she died?"

The doctor's face broke into a reassuring smile as he gently shook his head. "No, your baby did not suffer," he said. "For reasons no one in the medical field knows, her little heart just slowly stopped beating. There was no pain."

A weight was lifted from my heart as I heard those words. My little baby had just slowly and peacefully drifted away into the arms of Jesus. I thank God for the peace I have in knowing that she is truly with Abba Father, her Daddy God.

Dear friend,

God is watching over your little one. He treasures having your baby in heaven with Him! I pray this very thought would warm your heart and bring peace to your soul.

MOTHER'S DAY

You knit me together in my mother's womb.
—Psalm 139:13

$\mathcal{M}$other's Day—a day of so many mixed emotions.

The emptiness of the day is so consuming I can't get away from it. It's everywhere. Women with newborns in their arms on TV, pictured in store flyers, strolling into church—everywhere. And whose arms are aching and empty? Mine. I should have been one of those women with an infant in my arms today. Somehow, though, I feel as if the reality of having a baby slipped right through my arms, almost like a vapor. One day she was a part of me and the next she was gone. I want to cuddle that little life, but there is nothing, absolutely nothing, to cuddle.

There is a feeling of desperateness in my heart, but it is at this point I realize I must focus on what I do have instead of what I don't have. And I do have something! I may not be strolling into church or appearing in a family picture with a newborn in my arms; but, nevertheless, I do have a child. I am a mother. The moment conception took place I was blessed with the gift of a child and the title of "Mommy." Psalm 139 clearly states, "You knit me together in my mother's womb."

I am a mother of a little rose in heaven and nothing—absolutely nothing—will change that. And although I don't have my little rose in my arms today, I do have the comfort of knowing that a glorious day is coming when I will meet her and together as a family, we will spend eternity with Jesus.

Dear friend,

This is one of the hardest days to face with empty arms and an aching heart. It is normal to feel overwhelming grief and sorrow on Mother's Day. My prayer, though, is that you will not become swallowed in emptiness to the extent that you miss the honor of being a mother today and forget the hope of spending eternity with your child.

LISTEN TO MY CRY

The eyes of the Lord are toward the righteous,
and His ears are open to their cry.
—Psalm 34:15 (NASB)

I am constantly amazed at how many things are different in my life since Molly died. Some things are so obvious they stare me right in the face. Like the fact that I don't feel my baby move when I lie down at night. Or that I don't wear maternity clothes anymore. Other things, however, are seemingly insignificant until they catch me off guard. When that happens my emotions seem to go into a free spin, totally out of my control.

Last night, I walked into the church fellowship hall a few minutes early for a special meeting. People were gathered in small groups just chatting together. I was about to join a small group of ladies when I saw another woman approach them and playfully pat the swollen belly of a pregnant friend. A pang ripped through me and I turned and headed toward the restroom.

Such a small, seemingly insignificant thing—so why did it send my emotions reeling? To the casual onlooker, that pat was probably insignificant, but to me it was a powerful reminder that the life inside my womb was gone. The little pat a friend gives a pregnant woman is an acknowledgement of the life inside her. Friends don't pat my belly anymore because my baby is dead.

The world keeps on moving, but at times like these when I stop and weep for my baby, I take comfort in knowing Jesus is watching over me and He has stopped to listen to my pain.

Dear friend,

I know it hurts to feel like the rest of the world has brushed right by you. But remember, Jesus hasn't. My prayer is when you need to mourn the loss of your baby, you will know that His ears and heart are always open to your cry.

THE PLANS OF THE LORD

The plans of the Lord stand firm forever.
—*Psalm 33:11*

*H*ow many times will I question every detail of my life to determine how it may or may not have contributed to Molly's death?

"If I had called the midwife sooner … "

"If only I had not worked so hard that morning … "

"Why wasn't I more in tune to my body …?"

"Did that little bit of chocolate every afternoon cause problems … ?"

Through the prayers and reassurance from my husband, faithful friends, and a compassionate doctor, I am learning I am not to blame for Molly's death. Psalm 33 tells me, "The plans of the Lord stand firm forever." I can know, as a conscientious mother, there was nothing I did or could do to blow the plan God had for me or little Molly.

Dear friend,

Don't become obsessed with the "if only" thoughts that often occupy your mind. As a loving mother, you cared for your baby. You are not to blame for your baby's death. We don't always understand the big picture, and, as Christian mothers, we do not have the ability, even if we wanted, to mess up God's plan for our lives and the lives of our babies. I don't understand how or why God dictates or allows things to work out the way He does, but I know in my heart He loves us dearly and He alone is the Master Planner. I pray you would rest in that truth today.

SITTING ON THE SIDELINE

I will never leave you nor forsake you.
—Joshua 1:5

*M*y friend asked me yesterday how I felt when other women told me they were pregnant. The truth is the initial news excites me. It's just the ongoing events surrounding the pregnancy that hurt. Pregnant mothers all talking about weight gain, morning sickness, nursery decor, and doctor visits combined with the sight of swelling bellies all create an ache deep inside my heart.

I want to be a part of the excitement and anticipation that creates a common bond among pregnant women. It's a bond similar to that of a sports event, where all the players work as a team to offer support and encouragement throughout the duration of the game. Instead, however, I feel as if I've been disqualified from the game and left to watch from the sideline. I'm not even sure who disqualified me; nevertheless, the feelings are there, and they hurt.

Satan would love for me to believe that God

has disqualified me from that game and even from His love. It takes a conscious effort for me to reject his lies and hang on to the truth of God my Father. His promise, "I will never leave you nor forsake you," helps me realize that when I feel the loneliness of sitting on the sidelines, God is sitting right beside me.

Dear friend,

I thank God for His promise that He will never leave us nor forsake us. My prayer for you today is that even in the midst of feeling so alone, God would reveal Himself to you. I pray He would fill your heart with comfort and your mind with peace so you can rest in Him.

THROUGH THE
EYES OF A CHILD

How great is the love the Father has lavished on us,
that we should be called children of God!
And that is what we are!
—1 John 3:1

$\mathcal{A}$ few days ago my little boy, Matthew, and I were working in the garden. While digging in the dirt, Matthew found a small toy I had never seen before. "I wonder where that came from?" I asked out loud.

Matthew looked at the dirty toy in his hands and replied, "It's from Molly. She dropped it down from heaven just for me."

My heart melted as I realized the amazing perspective my four-year-old son had about his little sister. He truly believed she loved him and cared for him so much that she dropped a gift for him to find.

We have so much to learn from the minds of children, but we have even more to learn from their hearts.

Dear friend,

   Our Heavenly Father tells us that we are His precious children. I pray God would help you and I both to become more childlike. Always trusting, always hoping, and always believing.

FLYING SOLO

*Each of you should look not only to your own interest, but
also to the interests of others.*
—Philippians 2:4

 G rief is neither simple nor predictable.
And one place where the grief process is especially complicated is in a marriage relationship. The differences between a husband and
wife are never ending. In our marriage, I need
to work through the grief process with a companion, and Brian needs to work through it
alone. I am thankful Brian is there for me as a
compassionate spouse, constantly offering the
embrace of his arms, the strength of his faith
and the encouragement of his words. Curiously
though, I feel as if I rarely get to offer these
same gifts to Brian in return.

When it comes to this journey of grief, I
have accepted the fact that Brian prefers to fly
solo. At first I was hurt and insulted, thinking
that he didn't need me the way I needed him.
I felt as if I had nothing to offer his aching
heart. As I continue to watch his flight, however, I see that while he may not need the same

support system I do, he still needs a valuable gift from me—the gift of space. Space to grieve at his own pace and in his own way, without needing to conform to my style of mourning. Among many things, it means allowing him to spend several hours in quiet when he wants to work on a project. It means allowing him to visit Molly's grave without reporting to me first. And it means allowing him to hear from God without always needing to share the new insights with me.

By giving Brian the freedom to fly solo, he is better able to meet my need for companionship. So instead of heading for a crash landing, we have begun flying in a whole new formation. No doubt we will encounter storms and turbulence along the way, but one of these days we will break out into blue skies. When we do, we will never look at the world or each other in the same way again.

Dear friend,
There is no manual for grief, although it sure would make things easier! Consider your spouse's

needs during his grief process. Many men need space to work through their emotions. If this is the case in your marriage, allow your husband the freedom to grieve apart from you so that in turn he has the strength to grieve with you.

Am I Normal?

Oh Lord, you have searched me and you know me.
—Psalm 139:1

I laugh, I cry, I smile, I frown. I hurt and I heal, I rejoice and I mourn. Up and down, back and forth. I go weeks and weeks feeling strong and then weep over a TV commercial advertising Kodak film. I feel like a conqueror, then two days later I feel like I have been conquered. I feel excitement as I celebrate the birth of a friend's baby, then I'm caught up in unexpected grief during a children's program at church. I'm all mixed up and yet I am all together.

Am I normal? I ask myself. But who knows what normal is anyway? I read material on grief; I listen to the counsel of friends; I search God's Word and seek His guidance. And as a result, I have come to one conclusion. I feel the way I feel, and that is OK.

Dear friend,

Please be assured there is no normal way to feel after the loss of a baby. If your days have turned into weeks of deep, dark depression you must seek professional help. But don't add additional weight to your heavy load by constantly wondering, Am I normal? *Keep the lines of communication open between you and your husband and a few close friends. Then rest in the reassurance you can indeed feel the way you feel.*

WE SEND YOU WITH A NAME

Fear not, for I have redeemed you,
I have summoned you by name; you are mine.
—Isaiah 43:1

A few nights ago, my daughter came to me holding a torn piece of tablet paper with a simple drawing. "These are your babies in heaven," she explained, pointing to three little bundles. "The one in the middle is Molly. What are the names of these two babies?" she asked, referring to the two babies we had lost to miscarriages. Stumped by the question, I replied, "Well, they don't have names." She then exclaimed, "They don't have names? Why not? They need a name."

Such a true statement, but how could I explain to this tiny child that when we lost these babies few people even acknowledged their little lives. No one told us we could name our babies. We didn't even know if they were boys or girls. We were expected to move on with life. And we did—sort of. Truth is, I always felt guilty for not giving those little lives their names.

Suddenly I said, "Megan, would you and Matthew each like to name one of our babies?" Her blue eyes grew huge at the thought of being given such a grown-up task. "Matthew!" she screamed. "Mommy said we can each name one of the babies!" That evening we made a list of names and prayed about the decision. Megan, wanting a sister, chose the name Madison. Matthew, in typical boy fashion, wanted a brother and chose the name Mitchell.

It was as if God guided us through the process simply to bless our family. What a testimony brought on by a small child who knew in her heart that every child deserves a name! Now we talk often about Molly, Madison, and Mitchell in heaven. Giving the babies a name has also helped me work through some of the grief that had been hidden away in my heart for more than eight years.

Dear friend,

Many mothers, fathers, and siblings have found a true blessing in naming their little baby no matter at what stage of pregnancy or birth the loss occurred. Not every family feels comfortable doing this, but there can be a certain healing that takes place when you send your baby with a name you have chosen for just him or her. I pray you would feel a clear peace from God as you seek Him for guidance in this decision.

A VISITOR FROM HEAVEN

by Twila Paris

A visitor from heaven,
If only for a while.
A gift of love to be returned.
We think of you and smile.

A visitor from heaven,
Accompanied by grace.
Reminding of a better love
And of a better place.

With aching hearts and empty arms,
We send you with a name.
It hurts so much to let you go,
But we're so glad you came.
We're so glad you came.

A visitor from heaven,
If only for a day.
We thank Him for the time He gave,
And now it's time to say,
We trust you to the Father's love,
And to His tender care.
Held in the everlasting arms,
And we're so glad you're there.
We're so glad you're there.

With breaking hearts and open hands,
We send you with a name.
It hurts so much to let you go,
But we're so glad you came.
We're so glad you came.

THE LANGUAGE OF LOVE

The good man brings good things out of the good
stored up in his heart.
—Luke 6:45

Men are different than women. It's a simple fact I have known all of my adult life, especially since I have been married. I know, without question, Brian loves Molly just as much as I do. He just expresses it differently. In many ways, it's like we both speak a different language. Therefore, I have a choice to make. I can either try to force Brian to speak my language or I can seek to see and hear the beauty in his.

Brian doesn't talk, write, or cry about our little girl on a daily or even a weekly basis like I do. He doesn't sit down on the edge of the bed with her Keepsake Memory Box, gently fingering the only tangible mementos of her life. He doesn't write in a journal, glue pages in a memory album, or play lullabies over and over again. But by learning Brian's language of love, I have been able to look back over the past months and see the testimony of his love for Molly through his simple yet deliberate actions. He said, "I love you," as he skillfully crafted her tiny white casket and meticulously inscribed Molly's initials in the top. He said, "You are special," as he carefully planted and trimmed her memorial tree. He said, "I'll miss you, sweet doll," as he laboriously dug her tiny grave and led the funeral procession to the cemetery carrying her casket. And he said, "You'll always be in my heart," as he set a white cross in our flower garden.

The language of love that flows from an individual is a sacred gift. It has the power to change lives if we would only learn to listen with our hearts.

Dear friend,

In the noise-filled world around us, it is so easy to miss the most precious words, "I love you." I pray you would listen, not with your ears but with your heart, to the powerful messages that are flowing from the heart of your spouse. Listen carefully, for the message you hear will stay in your heart and mind forever.

MERELY A PAWN?

And we know that God causes all things to work together
for good to those who love God.
—Romans 8:28 (NASB)

$\mathcal{A}$s the months passed since our baby's death, I tried to figure out why the whole thing happened. I had lost two babies to miscarriages before and now I had lost Molly to a stillbirth. I remember several people telling me how the death of my baby actually helped them work through a particular loss in their own life. Another person said they felt they had been drawn closer to God through our loss. One person even explained how his marriage was stronger than ever because God had convicted him during this time of grief.

For quite awhile I felt angry with God for seemingly using Molly's life like a pawn in a chess game. He put her on the front line and allowed her life to be forfeited so that others "could grow closer to Him" or "heal from past hurts" or even "build a stronger marriage." Why did my baby's life have to be lost so that others could benefit? I confessed my struggle to our pastor who in turn shared some insights with me.

Molly died, not because Satan killed her and not because God chose to end her life. She died because we live in a sinful, fallen world where disease, sickness, and death run rampant. But when Molly died, bitterness could have wreaked havoc in the lives of everyone around us. Satan was prowling like a lion ready to devour and destroy our marriage, our relationships with others, and most important, our relationship with God. God did not take Molly's life. He chose, however, to use the death of our child to draw people closer to Him, heal past hurts, and even restore relationships.

Wow! What an amazing revelation! For the first time, I truly understood Romans 8:28. God allows tragedies to come into our lives, but He does not create them. He is a sovereign God and causes everything to work out for the good of those who have the courage to trust Him.

Dear friend,

I pray for the protection of you and your family so that bitterness and Satan's plans to harm you will fail miserably. May God take your loss and your pain and use it for good, for so He promises to do for those who love Him.

THE SANCTITY OF LIFE

For our struggle is not against flesh and blood,
but against the rulers, against the authorities,
against the powers of this dark world and against
the spiritual forces of evil in the heavenly realms.
—*Ephesians 6:12*

*T*oday is Sanctity of Life Sunday. A day set aside for the nation to focus on the sanctity of life. The dictionary defines sanctity as that which is holy or sacred. I think of our two miscarried babies and our stillborn little girl and their short life in my womb. These two words, holy and sacred, create a feeling of awe in my soul.

At the same time, a surge of anger charges through my veins as I read the statistics in my church bulletin. This year 1,300,000 unborn children will lose their lives. As a mother, I had fought desperately to preserve the lives of my three unborn children, and here are 1,300,000 mothers who are making the choice to kill their babies. The struggle inside my mind is great as I try to comprehend the horror of these vast numbers. Don't they know? Don't they understand how sacred the little baby is that is growing inside their womb? Don't they understand the awesomeness of this creation? Why was I denied my treasured baby and yet they purposely choose to throw theirs away like a piece of trash? I just don't understand.

Dear friend,

The spiritual forces of evil influence the choices many mothers make. They don't understand because they don't know Jesus. I pray as you work through the emotions surrounding this day you would be able to praise God for protecting you in this spiritual war. Because you know Jesus, you are not deceived by the powers of this dark world. Instead, you know in your heart and understand in your mind the true sanctity of your baby's life.

ABORTED ...
AND NO ONE CARED

Your eyes saw my unformed body ...
how precious to me are your thoughts, O God!
How vast is the sum of them!
—Psalm 139:16-17

*I*t is a picture that will be forever etched in my mind. I can see it as clearly today as I could some twenty years ago in junior high school. It is the picture of a tiny dead baby lying in a heap inside a small plastic bucket. The baby had been aborted. This graphic photograph was on the inside of a pro-life pamphlet intended to force people to see and deal with the reality of abortion. It was a photograph more horrific than anything I had seen before.

Throughout the years, conversations and debates centering around abortion would always bring that picture to the very forefront of my mind, followed by a sickening numbness that would settle in the pit of my stomach.

Now years and years later, the picture is in my mind again. This time, though, the horror is replaced by overwhelming sorrow. When I delivered Molly, she was stillborn at five months. But, oh, how we loved her! We tenderly wrapped her in a hand crocheted blanket the hospital had given to us and held her for nearly six hours. We took her footprints, we filled in her baby book, and collected little mementos from her birth. My husband and two children made her a tiny white casket with her initials inscribed on the top. We had a funeral service for her and grieved with family and friends. We made up a scrapbook, wrote in a journal, and, just before Christmas, we placed a beautiful little headstone on her grave. We loved our baby more than words could say.

But the little baby in that bucket had nothing because no one cared. No loving arms to wrap around him, no memento to keep his memory alive. I feel such a deep, deep sorrow for that little baby. To be perfectly created, secretly knit together in his mother's womb, only to be killed and dumped in a bucket for the trash. Oh, how my heart hurts for him!

Dear friend,

Your grief in the loss of your child reveals the fact that you know the truth. The truth that life is precious and is meant to be treasured, cared for, and loved. Let us give praise to God that He has shown us that truth and He holds the lives of precious babies in heaven, safe and sound, loved and cherished.

An Evaluation
of the Heart

Test me, O Lord, and try me,
examine my heart and my mind.
—Psalm 26:2

Our pastor said in his morning message that this verse was dripping with evaluation. It's true. Test, try, and examine both the heart and the mind. Total exposure with nothing hidden. When I prayed that prayer and asked God to evaluate my heart and mind, I was sickened by the areas of darkness He revealed. Somehow, over a period of time, a certain hardness had crept into my heart, and, in the process, an element of my compassion and tenderness had been pushed out. In particular, I reflected on my attitude toward women who had chosen to have abortions. I hated their sin, which is justifiable, but now I had begun to hate them as well.

At that point, I realized I had chosen to hang on to a portion of my grief after Molly's death, instead of handing it totally over to God. The result was an ugliness in my heart with which I had grown very comfortable. As I asked God to forgive me and cleanse my heart, I felt a glimpse of my compassion and mercy returning for those women. I want to get back to the place where I can hate the sin of abortion, but love the mothers as Christ does. I'm not there yet, but I'm closer to that desire than I was a short time ago.

So while Psalm 26:2 drips with evaluation, I found it has the power to cleanse and drench a person with freedom as well.

Dear friend,

Bearing the weight of grief and heartache does not justify the ugliness we may have allowed to creep into our hearts. Maybe you are struggling with your response to your husband and friends. Maybe it's your doctor, pastor, or even yourself. Whatever it may be, ask the Lord to evaluate the very core of who you are as a wife, friend, mother. If you allow Him, He will cleanse your heart and mind while drenching you with a new and glorious freedom.

FIGHTING BACK WITH THE POWER OF PRAYER

*The effective prayer of a righteous man
can accomplish much.*
—James 5:16 (NASB)

During the first weeks after losing our baby, we felt the power of prayers that were lifted up to heaven on our behalf. We knew, perhaps for the first time in our lives, what it really meant to be carried in the arms of Jesus. As we look back over those first days, when we were stumbling around in shock, we can see how prayers sustained our health, our spirits, and our hope.

After the "shock wave", however, we were faced with the journey of grief. A journey that seemed to lead into utter darkness. I remember thinking, "What are we going to do? How are we going to make it?" God sent a message through a friend, who shared with me the fact that God never intended for us to walk this journey alone. The Church, the Body of Christ, was to walk with us. But before the Church could walk with us, we had to let them know we needed them. That task required honesty, openness, trust, and vulnerability. Starting with close friends and our pastoral couple, we shared our hearts and asked them to pray for our family. And they did.

Now, months later, we continue to ask close friends to pray for our family and especially our marriage. Grief is hard work, but we are committed to fighting for our marriage instead of becoming another divorce statistic. We see God's hand of protection on us, and we know that He is honoring and blessing our marriage. We praise Him for restoring what has been lost and doing exceedingly more than we could have hoped or asked for.

Dear friend,

No matter how strong you or your marriage may be, you must depend on the Body of Christ to intercede for you, your spouse, your marriage and your family. Share your journey with them and allow them to lift you up before the throne of God.

AGAINST THE ODDS

He restores my soul.
—Psalm 23:3

Each year over 800,000 women lose babies to miscarriage, stillbirth, and early infant death. When people find out that I have experienced both miscarriage and stillbirth, they often tell me about their own loss of a child. It weighs heavy on my heart to hear so many women share how their marriages were either destroyed or deeply wounded as a result. Communication breaks down and walls go up in so many relationships.

I did some research and found that the second leading cause of marriage breakup is a tragic event in the lives of the husband and wife. The loss of a child to miscarriage, stillbirth, or early infant death is listed as one of those tragedies. I am sure there are many factors that determine if the marriage is going to fail or not. One of those factors, I believe, is deciding how hard we are willing to fight for our marriage. The tragedy of losing a child can indeed destroy a marriage, but God promises that it doesn't have to. Death steals so much from people, but our Almighty God has the power to restore all that has been lost—and more!

Dear friend,

The word restore means "to bring back to original condition that which has been damaged." What an awesome promise from the Word of God. And who will restore your soul where it has been damaged? The Lord and only the Lord. My prayer is that you would surrender your heart, your dreams, and your marriage to God so He can begin the delicate but powerful process of restoration.

Hold Me Close

The eternal God is your refuge,
and underneath are the everlasting arms.
—Deuteronomy 33:27

A close friend of mine is pregnant and due only a week and a half after Molly should have been born. After miscarrying her first baby, Kim and her husband tried for an entire year to become pregnant. I was so happy when her pregnancy test came back positive. Her dream of having a family is going to come true.

Yesterday she spoke with a sparkle in her eye and showed me the spot on her swollen belly where she could feel her baby's foot. At that moment I was as excited as Kim. The rest of the day, however, my heart was heavy. I, too, wanted to feel the bump of my baby's foot or elbow.

Sometimes late at night when everyone else is asleep, I lie awake in bed trying to imagine my baby moving under the weight of my hand. But no amount of imagining will bring her back.

My womb is now silent and still. My heart aches because I miss my little girl. My arms ache because they will be empty on my baby's due date.

Dear friend,

Late at night when your heart cries and your arms ache for the precious little baby you have lost, I pray you would feel God's arms wrap around you. Know He wants to hold you close and love you to sleep.

A Hollow Due Date

The Spirit helps us in our weakness. We do not know
what we ought to pray for, but the Spirit himself
intercedes for us with groans that words cannot express.
—Romans 8:26

$\mathcal{A}$s I looked out across the great expanse of the Chesapeake Bay, I couldn't help but feel small and alone. Today was my scheduled due date. My belly should have been huge with the anticipation of contractions starting any minute. Instead, I felt an incredible emptiness inside, both physically and emotionally.

"I love you, Molly. I know so very little about you, but you were and still are my little girl." My words were answered only by the rhythmic lapping of the waves on the sand. My due date, but both my womb and my arms were empty. The ache in my heart was too much to bear. I wanted to pray but could not find the words. I closed my eyes and sat in silence. No tears came but my heart wept in quiet grief.

Dear friend,

Oh, how it hurts! The emptiness is so over-whelming. But during this time, I pray you would not struggle to find the right words to pray, because there simply are none. Instead, be assured the Holy Spirit hears and understands your every groan, your every cry, your every tear.

ONE DAY AT A TIME

by Marijohn Wilkin and Kris Kristofferson

I'm only human, I'm just a woman,
Help me believe in what
I could be and all that I am.
Show me the stairway I have to climb.
Lord, for my sake teach me
to take one day at a time.

One day at a time, sweet Jesus,
That's all I'm asking from you.
Just give me the strength to do every day
What I have to do.
Yesterday's gone, sweet Jesus,
And tomorrow may never be mine.
Lord, help me today, show me the way
One day at a time.

Do you remember
when you walked among men?
Well, Jesus, you know
if you're looking below,

It's worse now than then.
Pushin' and shovin' crowdin' my mind.
So for my sake teach me
to take one day at a time.

One day at a time, sweet Jesus,
That's all I'm asking from you.
Just give me the strength to do every day
What I have to do.
Yesterday's gone, sweet Jesus,
And tomorrow may never be mine.
Lord, help me today, show me the way
One day at a time.

THE MEMORY TREE

He will be like a tree firmly planted by streams of water …
The Lord knows the way of the righteous.
—Psalm 1:3, 6 (NASB)

*M*y husband and I recently spent part of an afternoon walking up and down the aisles of a landscape nursery looking for the perfect tree to plant in memory of Molly. I had some ideas as to what kind of tree I wanted, but nothing seemed to suit my heart. After walking around for quite some time and listening to the manager explain the pros and cons of different trees, I began to feel discouraged. *Maybe this whole thing was just a silly idea,* I thought. *Why did I ever think I could find a tree to adequately reflect the memory of my little girl?*

Just when I had resigned myself to the fact that the whole mission was a failure, we walked around the corner of the building. There in front of me was the exact tree I had envisioned. Only six feet high, this ornamental Snow Fountain Weeping Cherry was full of long graceful branches. Each of the branches was in turn covered with beautiful white flower petals. The branches swayed and the flower petals fluttered in the gentle afternoon breeze. It looked like it was covered with lace, so graceful and so delicate. It truly reflected the memory of Molly.

That beautiful tree is now in our yard, appropriately planted right in front of our play area. Now when I watch my children playing in the sunshine, the memory of Molly is right there with them.

Dear friend,

A tree firmly rooted offers strength and stability. At the same time, it offers many smaller gifts that often go unnoticed. Gifts of cool shade, rustling leaves, even a graceful dance on a breezy evening. I pray that you would see God as that strong tree in your life, offering you strength and stability as well as memories, treasures, and reminders of your tiny baby.

FEARFULLY AND
WONDERFULLY MADE

For you created my inmost being;
you knit me together in my mother's womb.
I praise you because I am fearfully and wonderfully made.
—Psalm 139:13, 14

*A*s I think about the day I gave birth to my little girl, my mind is filled with many good memories. I think about the six hours my husband and I spent holding our daughter, trying to memorize every one of her precious little features. Her tiny fingernails and little red lips were both shaped like our daughter Megan's.

Throughout the evening we asked close family and friends to come and hold our little girl, just as we would have had she been born at nine months. It was a special time as we watched them examine her feet, toes, fingers, and little tiny ears. We knew this would be the only time we would ever have to get to know our little Molly here on earth.

While holding my little girl snugly in her crocheted blanket, her little face made me smile.

At five months old, her thin little body and shiny red skin didn't qualify her for a Gerber-baby contest, but she was my little Molly and to me she was beautiful.

Dear friend,

We had lost two babies to miscarriages five years before Molly was born. And, although we never had the privilege of seeing those babies, I do know, just like Molly, they were fearfully and wonderfully made. I don't know how old your baby was when he or she died. No matter what the age, I pray that you would know your baby was and is a beautiful creation, fearfully and wonderfully fashioned by the Master's hand.

TROUBLING THOUGHTS

You understand my thoughts from afar.
—Psalm 139:2 (NASB)

Each week since Molly died I seem to struggle with a new troubling question. Sometimes, after much thought and prayer, I come to some kind of a conclusion about my question. Many times, however, my questions go unanswered.

Lately, I've been wrestling with the question of whether or not Molly knows and loves me as her mommy. I know and love Molly as my daughter. My two other children share a bond with me as their mommy. But what about Molly? As my baby grew in my womb for five months, she heard my heart beat, my breathing, and my voice. Now those comforting sounds are gone. Does she miss them?

Molly lives in heaven now, and I know she would never want to leave that wonderful place for earth, but does she long to meet her mommy one day? Or does she not even know I exist?

Some of my questions will never have answers, but somehow that doesn't stop me from wondering.

Dear friend,
God understands the thoughts and questions that eat away at your heart. You can trust Him with those thoughts. You can trust Him with those questions. Most of all, I have learned, you can trust Him with your child.

PRECIOUS TO ME, O GOD

How precious to me are your thoughts, O God!
How vast is the sum of them!
Were I to count them,
they would outnumber the grains of sand.
—Psalm 139:17, 18

$\mathcal{P}$salm 139 has become such a vital part of my healing journey. The chapter refers to the time when David was but a mere embryo in his mother's womb. Yet while in that early stage, David states without question that God knew him intimately. Before his mother even knew she was pregnant, God was thinking precious thoughts about that "lump of tissue" in the womb. And God cares about all human life in the same way. So many precious thoughts from God were directed toward my babies that if I were to count them they "would out-number the grains of sand."

My little girl asked recently, "Mommy, how high do numbers go?" My answer was "They go on and on forever!"

Wow! God's thoughts towards babies are endless! He cares about Molly! He cares about my two babies that miscarried. He cares about my husband, my children, and me. He cares!

Dear friend,

Maybe you feel as if the world, even your family and friends, don't recognize the preciousness of your baby's life. Be encouraged because God cares! He knows how precious your baby is to you because he or she is so precious to Him.

A CHRISTMAS LONGING

Praise be to the Lord, to God our Savior,
who daily bears our burdens.
—Psalm 68:19

*T*he excitement and laughter of Christmas surrounded me. I watched wrapping paper fly off packages and heard screeches of delight follow as a niece or nephew discovered their coveted gift. It truly was a time of celebration. I felt blessed to be a part of it all. For a short moment, though, I became lost in my own thoughts. This was to have been my baby's first Christmas, and it's tradition in our family that the new grandchild always received his or her first Christmas ornament from Grandma. A twinge of sadness crept in as I thought about what would have been, then I focused my thoughts once again on the celebration around me.

A little while later I was handed a small gift. The tag said it was from my mom and dad. Not giving the contents a whole lot of thought, I pulled back the tissue paper, and the sight that met my eyes sent an instant shiver through my body. A gold crescent moon cradled a baby girl on a tiny pink pillow. Gold stars and beautiful delicate rose buds surrounded the sleeping infant. Printed neatly above the baby in a puffy cloud was the name Molly Dawn. I stared at the ornament and couldn't believe how perfectly it reflected my little girl. I looked up and saw my mom and my sister watching me with tears in their eyes.

My baby had not been forgotten on her first Christmas.

Dear friend,

I know you are struggling with a certain sadness during your baby's first Christmas. But please remember that God is a God who not only wants to bear our burdens, but He wants to give us special delights as well. My prayer is that you would find a tangible way to capture the spirit of Christmas and the memory of your baby together. It is amazing how God can and will use this keepsake to bring healing, not only this first Christmas, but also in the Christmases to follow.

THE GIFT OF A CHILD

For unto you this day, in the city of David,
a Savior has been born; He is Christ the Lord.
—Luke 2:11

When we get away from the hustle and bustle of the man-made Christmas, we can allow ourselves to see the God-made Christmas. How marvelous to think that the first gift of Christmas was a child. Yes, the heaviness of my baby not being in my arms for her first Christmas is incredible. Yet I realize in the midst of my sorrow, I simply must look at the first gift God gave to me. He gave me a child, His Son. If I look at this Gift Child and toss it away because of my pain, I could very easily be forever lost in my own grief.

If in the midst of my grief, however, I accept this Gift Child from God, I will find hope, even joy, comparable to nothing else in this world.

Dear friend,

Grieve the loss of your baby and the emptiness of his or her first Christmas. But, I pray with all my heart you would not be so lost in your grief that you miss the first gift of Christmas. A baby. God's baby—sent for you so you could find joy in the present and hope for the future.

The Death of a Dream

The Lord is close to the brokenhearted
and saves those who are crushed in spirit.
—*Psalms 34:18*

*A*s I struggle to sort through my feelings since the death of my baby, I have begun to realize this journey will last until I am reunited with Molly in heaven. For me, this grief process involves more than dealing with my emotions surrounding her death. It is the continual process of working through the pain of broken dreams.

I dreamed about my baby since the time my pregnancy test came back with the little "+" sign. I dreamed about her physical appearance, her personality, her strengths and weaknesses, as well as her likes and dislikes. With the death of my baby came the death of all my dreams for her. I will never see Molly's first smile, her first tooth, or her first step. I will never be able to toss her in the air and listen to her giggle. I will never be able to walk her to Sunday school for the first time, put a Band-Aid on her skinned knee, or solve an argument between her and her brother. I will never watch as she steps off the school bus, participates in a sports program, or turns red when a certain boy's name is mentioned. I will never pray with her over a job interview, watch her daddy walk her down the aisle, or see her blossom into womanhood.

Broken dreams. They started with her death and they seem to go on forever. Perhaps the hardest one of all is knowing I will never hug her and kiss her good night because I have already kissed her good-bye.

Dear friend,

Oh, how we miss our babies and the simple dreams they would have fulfilled simply by being in our lives. I pray you would feel the Lord's closeness right now. Broken dreams will break your heart, but God will not let them break your spirit. Cling to the wondrous dream of spending eternity with your baby! I promise this dream will come true.

A CHILD OF THE KING

*You have received the spirit of adoption as sons by which
we cry out, "Abba! Father!" The Spirit Himself bears
witness with our spirit that we are children of God,
and if children, heirs also—heirs of God
and fellow heirs with Christ.*
—Romans 8:15-17 (NASB)

I have noticed how popular the topic
of heaven becomes when somebody dies.
Especially a child. Many people have the idea
that heaven is this vapor-filled fairy-tale land
where children and adults who have passed
away sprout wings and fly around on clouds
playing harps. Thus, the topic of angels often
emerges with comments such as "God must
have needed another angel, so He chose your
little baby," or "Now you have an angel in
heaven watching over you." While these comments are meant to bring encouragement, I
can't help but wonder where some people get
their teaching on heaven.

When my baby died she did not become
an angel. As a child of God she went to heaven
to live with her Abba Father, her Daddy God.

Having been adopted by God, she is now a joint heir with Jesus! Never mind the angels and clouds—she's a child of the King living in His kingdom!

Dear friend,

While angels play a crucial role in the world around us, I pray you would find comfort in knowing your child didn't become one of heaven's angels. Far better than that, your treasured baby is alive and well, living in a real place with a real King who has adopted her as His very own.

HAPPY BIRTHDAY, SWEET BABY

Yet this I call to mind and therefore I have hope:
Because of the Lord's great love we are not consumed,
for His compassions never fail.
They are new every morning;
great is your faithfulness.
—Lamentations 3:21–23

The sky was gray and cloudy, lending itself to a blah feeling. Winter was gone, but the cheerfulness of spring had not yet arrived. Still, there was an air of excitement beginning to mount as the children and I tied the final knots on our birthday-message balloons for Molly.

Earlier that day I had purchased a helium balloon for every member of our family. With the balloons bouncing along the ceiling of our living room, each of us worked to create the perfect message for Molly. Finally, we chose the note or picture that we liked the best and tied it to the string on our balloon.

To the person looking in from the outside,

this whole activity may have seemed silly or even a waste of time. I knew these balloons would not float through heaven's gates into Molly's hands. Instead they would probably pop after we lost sight of them or drift away and land in a farmer's field sometime that evening. There was a special feeling of inner healing as Megan, Matthew, and I worked together on this project. It generated memories and conversation about Molly's life in my womb and her life now in heaven. Although my children never saw Molly alive, there was no denying that they loved and cherished their baby sister. Their notes and crayon drawings clearly reflected that.

I explained to the children that the balloons would not really reach heaven, but that this was a tangible way for us to remember Molly and celebrate her birthday. My four-year-old, however, already had the solution figured out. "They don't need to go to heaven, Mommy; the angels will read the messages and tell Molly all about them."

I felt those familiar tears filling my eyes and replied, "You know what Matthew? I bet you're exactly right."

Standing in the backyard, we shouted a countdown and released our balloons. As we watched the balloons sail higher and higher above the rooftops and trees, Matthew and Megan simply could not contain themselves. Jumping up and down they waved and screamed with delight. "Happy birthday, Molly! We love you!"

When the tiny dots of color disappeared from our view, Matthew spotted the neighbor boy and shouted, "Shawn, guess what? We just wished my baby sister 'Happy birthday!' and guess where she lives? In heaven!"

Dear friend,

My prayer is that you would feel a certain spirit of celebration as you remember your baby's birthday. I know the pain is strong, but don't let that pain steal the joy, memories, and healing this day can bring.

O LORD, I PRAY

How wide and long and high and deep is the love of Christ.
—Ephesians 3:18

Lord Jesus, you are so good to me. In my anger, you show me never-ending mercy. In my confusion, you show me abundant grace. In my sorrow, you show me constant compassion.

Lord, I pray that somehow I would grasp how wide and long and high and deep the love is that flows from your heart. May I not turn away from that love. May I only lift my eyes to see Your face, knowing that because of Your boundless love You are able to do more than I could ever ask, hope for, or imagine.

Father God, please bless me. Bless my family and all those who are walking this journey with us. May your face shine upon us and give us peace.

In Your precious name,
Amen

Dear friend,

God loves you so much. It doesn't matter what you have said or done, He will not withdraw His unfailing love. I pray you would find a quiet place to kneel before the God of the universe. Ask Him to bless your future and allow Him to lift you into His loving arms.

BUT JOY COMES
IN THE MORNING

Tears may last for a nighttime,
but joy comes in the morning.
—Psalm 30:5

I remember so vividly this verse from Psalms being prayed over our family after Molly died. "Tears may last for a nighttime, but joy comes in the morning." This verse gives the assurance of the grief passing or lasting only for a time. With the heaviness of Molly's death lying on my heart, I honestly didn't see how the tears and grief would ever come too an end.

As I made my way through the highs and lows of this journey, however, I slowly began changing course without even realizing it. Over time my journey of grief took detours that led to hope and healing.

Then one Sunday morning, our pastor put a notice in our church mailbox calling attention to an orientation meeting for parents who might be considering adoption. We had always wanted to adopt and we felt a certain curiosity about the orientation meeting. Several weeks later, we found ourselves seated with many other couples, listening to the presentation regarding the adoption of little girls from China. Halfway through the meeting, all heads turned toward the door to see a couple approaching the group. In the man's arms, his seven-month-old little Chinese daughter kicked and squealed as she looked at the crowd. Brian and I simultaneously squeezed each other's hand. At that moment we knew we were being called to adoption. With the death of Molly constantly on our hearts, we felt a confirmation that our little girl would be the joy that comes in the morning.

Even though we didn't know who she was, what she looked like, or even what her name would be, our family loved our little "joy" from the time we started the adoption process. For the next year and nine months we filled out paperwork, completed a home study, had a fingerprint check, and received criminal clearance. We attended a workshop, read information updates, and completed more paperwork. We had endless fundraisers, wrote our life's story, got physicals, and completed still more paperwork. We waited and prayed through changes and delays from the Chinese government regarding our qualification for adopting. Our two precious children, Matthew and Megan, prayed tirelessly for their future baby sister.

To our delight, in the midst of the adoption process I became pregnant. I struggled almost daily with the fear of losing the precious baby in my womb. It took a conscious, deliberate decision to continually commit the life of our baby into the hands of Jesus. That commitment was tested to the extreme when I was admitted to the hospital with complications and had to be induced.

When our infant son entered the world alive, well, and hungry we rejoiced! What an incredible blessing to deliver, hold, and take home a baby after the stillbirth of Molly. We named our son Micah Nathaniel, which means "who is like the Lord" and "gift from God."

One month after Micah's birth, the agency called and gave us the news we had a little girl from China! We felt the confirmation of God's hand on the entire process since we received this call on the same day we had said goodbye to Molly just two years before. When the FedEx man brought the package containing her picture and background information, the children and I nearly plowed him over. We ripped open the folder and stared at the dear little face on the tiny photo. Two months later in a rundown office building in Changsha, China, Malia Joy Waltman was laid in her daddy's arms for the first time. A wide smile spread across her face the moment she heard his voice. The waiting and wondering were over. Our Joy had finally come.

Dear friend,

God watches over our families with the greatest of care, gently leading us through grief and on to hope and healing. He has a beautiful plan for all of us when we surrender ourselves, our emotions, our dreams, even our pain to Him. My dear friend, He loves you so much. Trust Him, lean on Him, and believe in Him. Because while tears may last for a nighttime, joy will come in the morning.

MEMORY IDEAS

Many mothers struggle with the intense emotions of having nothing after their baby has died. There are very few, if any, memories, pictures, or mementos. Women often have a desire deep in their hearts to celebrate, pay tribute, or remember the life of their baby, no matter how brief his or her stay on earth.

The following is a list of ideas specifically for the purpose of keeping the memory of your baby alive. Several ideas are especially helpful if you have other children because it gives them a tangible, nonthreatening way to remember their sibling. Create your own ideas or tailor fit any of these to meet your needs and the needs of the loved ones around you.

1. Write a letter to your baby. Share your heartache and sorrow as well as your dreams of heaven.

2. Make a memory box for your baby. Tuck any special mementos, letters, gifts, or cards in the box. Add items whenever you would like. (For example: Christmas, due date, Mother's Day, anniversary of his or

her death) Look through the box alone or with others to rekindle the memories of your baby.

3. Erect a cross or plant a tree, bush, or bulbs in your garden in memory of your baby.

4. For your baby's birthday, consider having a small birthday cake. Tie notes or pictures to helium balloons and then release them into the sky.

5. For any gift-giving holiday, purchase a gift in memory of your child. Make it personal by choosing a gift according to the sex and age that your child would be, had he or she not have died. Wrap your gift and then bless a needy child in memory of your baby.

6. When you are ready, consider organizing a small memorial garden at your church in memory of all the children who have died from miscarriage, stillbirth, or early infant death.

7. Choose an ornament in memory of your baby, possibly engraved or personalized with his or her name and birth date.

8. Hang a Christmas stocking for your baby and have family members tuck special notes or pictures inside.

9. Purchase or have someone make a rag doll in memory of your baby. Include the doll in family photos if you wish.

10. Stitch a nursery sampler for your baby.

11. Press a flower from your garden or flower shop reflecting the season your baby died. Tuck it in a keepsake box or make it into a bookmark for your Bible or another favorite book.

A Personal Note
From the
Author

HEART: For many months, following the death of my little girl, I lived life in fear—fear of grief, fear of the future, fear of loving again, and fear of losing again. I kept my hand over my heart the same way a child keeps his hand over a skinned knee, afraid of letting his loving parent tend his wound. Only when I stepped out in faith and took my hand off of my bleeding heart did I see how God in His goodness was waiting to take my hand and walk with me through my painful journey of grief.

SOUL: Psalms 30:5 tells us that "tears may last for a nighttime, but joy comes in the morning." That is not just wishful thinking, it is a promise from our Heavenly Father. He sees every tear we shed and grieves with us over the loss of our dream, yet along with His grace and compassion is the amazing power He has to take a heart filled with sorrow and tears and flood it with abundant joy.

MIND: *I'll Hold You in Heaven* by Pastor Jack Hayford provides biblical answers to the many questions mothers and fathers often ask following the death of their baby. **www.Remember.TheRoses.com** is home to a powerful prayer team, committed to praying for those who have suffered the loss of their precious baby.

STRENGTH: Celebrating the memory of a lost child, through precious keepsakes, special occasions, and eventually reaching out to others in grief brings tremendous strength to a broken heart.

Lord Jesus,

I ask that today, you would touch these broken hearts in a powerful way. I trust you to lift them up and bring them hope—the hope of heaven and the hope of seeing their baby again, but also the hope of joy that you will restore to their lives. Comfort them with the knowledge that their precious baby is safe in your arms and may they feel your presence, your power, and your peace. In Your name, Amen.

In the Father's love,

Dawn

A Rose in Heaven Ministries is committed to addressing the many painful and complex issues surrounding pregnancy loss and early infant death. In addition to this book, *In a Heartbeat*, the following have shown themselves to be powerful avenues of ministry.

In a Heartbeat Seminars

Based on her book, *In a Heartbeat*, author Dawn Waltman shares her journey of grief, hope and healing after losing two babies to miscarriages and her daughter to a stillbirth. While this seminar ministers to women who have experienced pregnancy loss, it is also designed to educate and equip the world around us to become part of the healing process instead of compounding the hurt in a grieving heart. This powerful presentation is appropriate for women's groups, churches, and community groups, or can be structured to address caregivers, pastors, counselors, and those serving in the medical profession.

Prayer Network Ministry

Prayer is, without a doubt, one of the most powerful means of ministering to those who are grieving the loss of a baby. This unique prayer network is comprised of many families and individuals who are committed to praying for hurting individuals as the ministry becomes aware of their losses. An e-mail list of grieving families is sent out every month to members of the prayer team who in turn hold up these broken hearts before the Lord and cover them with fervent prayer.

To request a brochure on the *In a Heartbeat* seminar or to find out more about the prayer network, please visit **www.Remember.TheRoses.com** or contact

Heart Rhymes and Roses
P.O. Box 83
Intercourse, PA 17534
Email: Remember@TheRoses.com